Flores

Mayra Flores

BookLeaf Publishing

India | USA | UK

Presentation by *BookLeaf Publishing*

Web: www.bookleafpub.com

E-mail: info@bookleafpub.com

First edition 2024

Para todas las luchistas, tercas y soñadoras

Table of Contents

Puentes*

I am the bridge
between my past
and our future
between the old world
and the new
between my abuelita's hornito
that heated her
tortillas de trigo that she
made between her weathered
hands to sell around town
to keep the many mouths
of her familia fed in El Alamo
after my abuelo was killed;
and my child's bass lessons, swift
fingers plucking out the sounds
of their heart, the
joy of exploring the Californian
desert together, unhindered,
disconnected from the
technology that distracts us
while connected
to the ancestor's triumphs
and heartache through
our own.

I am the bridge
between the bravery
of an abuela I never
met, who came here to
work, to help support
her family back in Mexico,
while my abuelo
struggled to keep the family
together, fed and comforted
while their mamá, with her
hands, calloused from a
life as a seamstress
provided for them from
El Norte
and the joy
on my small niece's
face as she rides her
bike along the Guadalupe
under the warmth of the sun
alongside her sissy and dad
her dark hair waving
behind her.

I am the bridge
between my mother's
sacrifice, her childhood left
behind to support and
forge a futuro for us all
through endless years of work

operating the heavy
machines that would
give birth to Silicon Valley, and
my father's sweat and tears
as he washed cars in the heat,
along Stevens Creek boulevard,
trading his blue collar and name tag,
striking out and stepping up,
as his own jefe en la pulga,
a second-hand paradise.

I am the bridge.

*First published in East Side Magazine, Ome
issue, April/May/June 2022*

Abuelita Mia

*"You crossed a border to give me life and every
day I ask myself what border do I need to cross
to pay you back for that sacrifice?" - Diana
Medina, Healing Out Loud*

Your watery eyes, now blurred
with cataracts, move toward
my direction, but see past me

Mijita, como estás, you ask in
a soft, broken whisper, you
reach out your thin, small hand
translucent skin now a tinted
memory of your golden days
spent under the sun, in el corral

I take your hand into mine and
smile with my heart, hoping the
warmth will reach you through
the cobwebs of dementia

Your salt and pepper hair is
pulled up into a tidy little bun
atop your head, a detail of
tenderness, courtesy of mi ama

Your daughter, the fourth eldest of
nine children, who shares your golden
skin and stoic demeanor through
the heartache and heartbreak
that life has brought forth

And me, your granddaughter you
still remember by name, tu Mayrita,
who you cared for, using your yerbas
buenas, yerbas santas, every time my
head - or heart - hurt.

Trenzas

6

Trenzas, trenzitas
my mother taught
me how to weave
the dark hair when
I was six, calloused
fingers pirouetting
folding our past,
La Patria, and her
favorite pozo santo
safely within the
thickness of my
hair, her dreams of
El Norte and the
rolling of her Rs
tucked in every
pocket of these
braids, where no one
could strip away,
gentrify or bleach out
her pride and the grief
of leaving behind
her father's bones and
the water haven of La Concha
I cannot see
her face as she folds

hair over hair, memories
along that third lock,
but I listen as she narrates
what she's doing
like quiet prayers
for only god, and me.

Hermosa

My daughter
is shedding her skin
inch by inch
year by year
a dried-up husk,
hojas de tamal
that no longer fits,
no longer aids
in her search for self

Verdades susurradas.

Inconsequential
these pieces
she leaves strewn
room to room
like the name I gave her,
like the gender
assigned to her,
breadcrumbs
to who she truly is,
who she is becoming

The light shining through
forcing apart this shell

Respira.

Desahógate.

Desahógate mi amor.

With every wriggle, every crack,
as she pushes forward with
every smile, every scale
peeling off all that she's
outgrown,
every truth now a
tabloid headline in the trash

En plena vida.

She stands up straight
a full head above me
runs her fingers through
her long dark locks

Como agua corriendo.

Pushing past boulders,
nothing can slow her down
breaking away
at this god-given damn.

She's glowing.
She's breathing.
She's mine.
She's ours.
She's no one's.

Hermosa.

East Side Presente*

I am the struggle
the heartache
the headache

I am the success
the joy
the celebration

I am the color
so dark
so deep
provocatively showing up
showing out
standing proud

I am the sacrifice
of so many immigrants
of mothers
of fathers
of abuelitas and ninos

I am the fruit
of their labor
their laughter
their tears

I am everything
that makes you love us
fear us
envy and deny us

I am.

*First published in East Side Magazine, Yei
issue, July/Aug/Sept 2022*

Artemisia Vulgaris

I sit inside this yurt
in a circle that flows
with people, heated
by the iron stove of
desire to unlock
mysteries and remedies
deep within the stems and stalks
of our local flora, touching
the past through heated teas
and simmering drink
that coat our insides
in healing and out loud
joy, these herbs from the earth
connect me to strangers
brought together by the
crashing waves of the Pacific
rushing water during a storm
to become a strong tincture
of medicine friends
natural bridges
bringing me closer
to my abuelita's remedios
eyes closed I can almost
breathe her in.

St. James

Caterpillars rain down from the trees
with every gust of wind,
landing on us, disoriented, writhing,
seeking out food, shelter,
each other.

Their black, soft bodies
undulating
with every step they take,
gossamer hairs extending from their
flexible spines
feeling us out -

Friends or foes?

I reach out with a fallen tree twig,
gently coaxing
encouraging a new path.
stubborn, he refuses, staying the course
along my black stockings.

Wonder

I wonder …

Do we make a place or does the place
make us? Mold us?

My body yearns for the ocean's waves
and the cold, overcast skies,

Just as it yearns for the heat of the sun
reflecting off the granite and quartz boulders
of the skin-cracking deserts,

And the intoxicating smells of the soft
Redwood bark-covered forest floors

Does the ocean spray need me to breathe it in
to validate its majesty?

Does the desert need my sweat
dripping down during a hike to
quench her thirst?

Does the forest need my wail to echo against its
flesh to validate its existence?

My parents did not teach me to love them
never told me that I needed them like
the seasons need the bees or the birds or
the clever squirrels collecting their seed
and redistributing them in their hidey holes

Each of these landscapes folding
into the other - the heat, the cold,
the wet and the dry,
satisfying my body's kaleidoscope of needs

I wonder …

Forged

I grew up in the shadows
of broken women

Women torn down
by the men in their lives
by the predators
by the charlatans
the manipulators
and possessors

Each action against them
each act of cruelty
attempting to make them
smaller and smaller

Disarming them to better
break instead, forging them
into flinty statues, shedding
their softness, their warmth
with every word, every blow

Becoming impervious to
their strikes, defiance burning
in their dark, light, clear eyes
stronger with

every battle, until only one
stood …

I grew up as their shadow.

When I Look At You

When I look at you
and your large, dark eyes
and lips that fold and shrink
and expand with your smile
the way your hands flutter
around you as you speak
just like your grandmother
just like your mother

When I look at you
and your large, dark eyes
I see the eyes of countless
people before you, before us,
across time and space
coming together in love
in commitment
in responsibility

When I look at you
and your large, dark eyes
I see how so many of us's
came together to create
another generation
continuing,
move forward,

toward the future

When I look at you
and your large, dark eyes
I see we, expanding
like the universe
the darkness and the light
star stuff left in our eyes
reappearing again and again
with every me and every you.

Brave

I looked up at the massive
boulders stacked upon
boulders, the prehistoric
mountains in front of me,
and my heart raced,
my chest tightened.

My mind played
every worst-case scenario
like a bad movie, over and
over again. I watched as
the heat rose
from the granite, like a
warning, and I took a step
back. Every time.

Until a slender hand
reached out, a smile
pierced the panic
and a voice said to me,
"Come on mom,
I've got you.
You can do this."

So I did.

The Source*

I always felt disconnected
from my neighbors and my friends
from the kids at my school
and the families on TV

A constant gap
a missing piece
a reminder of otherness

Ni de aquí, ni de allá.

Always grasping for the intangible
a feeling that left me like
a seed in the wind
looking back, not knowing where
we've been

The history books we read
in class talked about
generations of people
tied together by the
bonds of lineage

Communities of our Indigenous
peoples, connected to the

Earth, to the animals, to
each other

Averigualo.

I yearned for this connection.

My parents' severed roots
from their beloved México
the pozo santo where my mom
swam with her brothers
or La Plaza where my dad sold
fruta to the faithful after church

Replanted on unwelcoming soil
and thriving nevertheless
despite the trauma
always smiling, lifting me up

¡Mija, tú lo puedes tener todo!

The buds began to take
in the black asphalt below
the movie screens of
my beloved Pulga

The sun was still slumbering
when our orange van
drove up to our designated

space every weekend

The Filipino family
across the way would
always wave to us
as we set up, offering
a hand or a watchful eye

The White man's toddler
from the organic honey stand
would hobble over, arms
outstretched to give
my mom a messy hug

And the fruteros unpacking
their trucks, calling out
the prices, the quality
would always stop -

¡Buenos Días Don Jesús!

We grew together, on
those hot summer days
drinking agua de coco
while finishing pages
of homework alongside
the constant disconnect
from my peers

I found myself in
uncharted territory, once again
places my parents had never been
the halls of a university, the
cacophony of a newsroom, the
screaming silence of a boardroom

Thirty-six hours of my
body breathing, breaking
surrounded by mi mami,
mi hermana y mi prima
giving way to the fruit
that would connect us all
to this space

Dark eyes reflecting ours,
firmly rooted, their place
cemented in confidence
securely tethered to me.

Al fin, amanecieron nuestras raíces.

*First published in East Side Magazine, Nahui
issue, Oct/Nov/Dec 2021*

Contraria

If you say go
my feet become cement
in place, seeping down
toward the earth, hardened
roots gripping in the dark

If you say stay
I become a roadrunner
dashing toward the horizon
full sprint, body leaning forward
the length of my tail steadying

If you say no
my mind begins to swim
in reasons and arguments
proving you wrong

If you say yes
my arms cross against my chest
hugging myself safe
I step back, one leg then the other

If you say nothing
suddenly the vice in my chest
tightens, the butterflies begin
to stretch their wings and I'm
out of breath.

Wet Mornings with Lula

Like a delicate dancer
lifting legs up and down
Lula's wet paws
paint a pattern
the bottoms
of her feet,
round cushions, press
against the peeling layers
of red paint of my
front porch
by the time a coherent
direction is found,
the traces evaporate.

Alviso

I had to lose you
to find you,
the you that warmed
me in your presence
that made me laugh
with my belly, full of
joy and wonder and
peace, that pushed
me past that sharp
corner, to get to where
you already knew I
wanted to be.

I miss exploring the
hidden beauty of our
favorite local park,
the weightless feeling
of being free, arms out
along the rich smell
of anise that could
overpower, make you
sick if smelled too much
or too long, maybe that's
why you aren't here, why
so suddenly you left me (us).

Vicki

You were everywhere
and then you weren't
every classroom I stepped
in, new and exciting
became a little less shiny
when your shrill voice
pierced the silence

That ratty cowboy hat
and pink cowboy boots
ever-present in every
space you occupied
my eyes rolled reflexively
and I made a mental note
another place I couldn't
get away from you, another
subject I'd have to share

It was like this for years, a
campus so big, the population
of a small city, not big enough
to create the buffer I longed
for from you, even after I left
the universe was hellbent on
shoving you toward me.

You extended your pale hand, a
first greeting, an introduction to
someone I had already added to
my running list of characters
who need an arms-length and
white gloves, you were tenacious
and I gave in, we were inseparable

Your blonde to my brunette, your
long legs pushing you closer to
the sky, mine keeping me grounded
toward the earth, the images you
skillfully captured with your blue
eyes and round lens, bringing my
words and phrases, voices to life

We whispered secrets into the
locks of each other's hair,
laughed deep and full and
never felt alone, you fought
with and for me, and I dutifully
reciprocated, two lionesses
roaring and snarling, teeth
bared and claws out, no one
stood a fighting chance,
we were sisters

When my daughter was born
your heart softened and you
spilled over with warmth and
tenderness, you were there
at every turn, every shaky
step, every milestone and
she called you Tía, her tiny
hands reaching out to yours

We drove to the cold, to the
snow and the mountains to
search for something - the
three of us and my old dog
Lula - you had just had your
double mastectomy, your
stealth boobs gone but pride
and grit and tenacity still intact

There was something in the
air, tension and rage and we
absorbed it into our flesh and
bones, weariness mixing with
… some unknown substance
lashing out with claws and
fangs and tools meant to hurt
taking turns at being wounded

I cried outside, the cold air
threatening to freeze my lungs
you cried in the tub, your
underwear stained with period
blood, we held each other, then
boiled over again and cried.

We drove back in silence, the
landscape blurring around us
like the world just before you
pass out, it never came back
into focus

The pain and hurt weighed
heavy on us, pulling us down
threatening to drown us both
we averted our eyes from the
other, and sat in silence

When you chose to leave, I
wasn't even surprised, I
didn't stop you, didn't plead
my case, just watched you
close the door and walk away
you left us both, though I know
you meant only to leave me

My old dog has since died, I
had her euthanized in my
home to stop her hurting, we
all sat next to her, my daughter
and my cats - her family - so
she wasn't alone, but now you
too are dying and I can't bring
myself to see you again, lock
eyes once more in that space
you created long ago when you
wouldn't let up, let me go, leaving
me with hurt once again, tears
flowing and tears at my seams.

Daisy

The outline of a daisy
peeks from your right
shoulder blade, just
the empty shape, shadows
of what was or what can
be found if you dig deeper,
go past the deceptively
simple black inked
lines, curving seemingly
delicate across your pale
skin, but etched
deep, layers down
to ensure
permanency,
that odorless flower,
never withering
everlasting life,
boundless happiness
as it stands tall.

Breasts

The first time a woman
grabbed my breasts I
was standing in front of
a poker table. I was wearing
a brown dress with a deep V
plunging down like a diver.
It was so quick, I didn't really
get a chance to process and/or
enjoy it.

Her long thin hands, white
marble skin and a tan-colored
tattered bandaid around her
pointer finger from a shooting
injury, reached around me and
cupped from underneath.

A flash went off like when a
firework blows and she giggled. I
still have that photo somewhere on
my drive.

When we went to the doctor's
office, she tucked her blonde
hair behind her ear, pulled at her

fingers and asked me to grab the
boobs of various shapes and sizes
in the display case.
'Help me pick my new ones'
she said to me. I obliged, touching
and weighing, feeling and moving
each the way you do with silly putty
or kinetic sand, attempting to find
her own breasts to soon cup.

Break Up (Again)

I lose my cool around
people who are dying
grow stiff, wooden like
on a first date going
badly over warm salads,
well, actually, just
with her

The obnoxiously bright
light that shone in my
life, even when I'd pulled
shut the drapes, closed
the door, walked away
she shoved her way back
in, shoulder first, always in
my face

Burrowing deep in my
heart, impossible to pull
out like an arrow through
flesh or a metal hook
though the lip, risking
inflicting pain onto myself
she held on, as she does

Now, tumors in her brain
tumors in her spine, the
weight spilling away
like the alcohol leaving
her body that one New
Year's Eve, there's nothing
stopping it, stopping her
as she leaves her withered
body, burying herself deeper
in me.

Bob

My petite shadow,
my child's confidant
she used to prance
from one room to the next
a miniature gazelle

She had no patience
never skittish or shy
taking the pets and loves
instead of waiting on us
a monarch ruling our home

She came into our lives
like a tiny meteor
entering our atmosphere
seemingly out of nowhere
looking straight into our eyes
vocally demanding adoration

Yesterday, on the last day of
the year, she walked slow
haunches trembling, into a
corner, a forlorn yowl
lost in her home, inevitability

In His Garden

The heat from the
sun beats
down on my skin, my dress,
the navy blue cotton
shift swirls
around my
legs with every step
I take
to follow you.

Your hands are busy
working, pulling
and cutting, measuring and
pushing,
building a makeshift lattice
wall between us, flanking
swirling green vines
inching from the earth upwards,
the space between us still
visible.

Our fingers reach out,
gingerly lifting each
soft stretch of life, against the
nylon framework, guiding,

coaxing, convincing them to
find the openings and
hold on.

The Place No One Can See

We walked the isles of Walmart today
running through our list when
I took a turn down an unplanned aisle
'What are we looking for?' she asked
I didn't answer, just kept looking
we inched slowly down, until I spotted
what I was looking for, hanging above.

'Béisbol gloves?' she asked and I smiled
and grabbed two. She shook her head
walked ahead and complained.
We got back to the ranch and we put
them on, along with hats and sneakers.

'I'm not good at catching,' she said.
'I'm not good at throwing,' she said.
'I have bad depth perception,' she said.
'I'm not a sports person,' she said.

And on and on.

My muscle memory ran through its
catalog until it landed on how to throw
sometime around my fifth attempt
my kid narrating what went wrong

with each throw and catch
until she caught her first ball.

Her body straightened up and she smiled
another throw, then another catch
the talking had stopped and that smile
spread across her body
again, and again,
the crack of the leather with every
catch, the growth of that smile
leading me to that place no one can see,
the place she keeps deeply hidden,
the place only a few are privileged to
witness; her confidence.

Waiting Room

The soft lavender on the back
wall washes away the dark
outline of her body,

Long and lanky,
currently resting
leg up, heel on her knee,
black face mask
obscuring her expression,

Only her dark eyes looking
down, lashes gently raising
and lowering as she sends
the next text message,

While she waits on her monthly
injection, serum more magical
than that found in the fountain
promising youth; this fountain
promises to bring her closer
to her true self.

What Are You So Afraid Of?

The dissatisfying disappointment
falling flat
falling down
falling
falling
over my feet like a racehorse
toppling face first,
rider and all
to the dark ground …

A crunch of limbs, legs and faces
leaving the audience
breathless
afraid to assess the carnage
unable to look away
a roar erupting in emotional
release, eyes focused
filling with …

My falling
falling
falling down as my family,
their sacrifice, dreams and
desires of a better life
come tumbling down

with me, and still …

I get back up
ignore the pain
shooting down
my spine,
my heart,
bloody teeth,
matted hair
ego bruised
dust off
smile on my lips
nada pasa
swing my leg
sit up
adjust
my black docs
secure in the stirrups
take the reins …

I ride my parents' trauma
to the future, to the better
life they promised
themselves,
promised us,
the hunger,
the loss,
my grandmother
bleeding out as she

birthed her last child
my grandfather slumped
over his beloved horse
brains and blood dripping
my parents' adolescent
drive, escape, to El Norte
their panting hot
breath always in my ear
whispering, reminding …

They ride my confidence,
identity and self-worth
my glistening brown skin
copper sweat in the sun,
muscles breaking,
whipping me with
immigrant guilt
first-born guilt
Catholic guilt
female guilt
guilt
to go faster
and faster
faster
to that brass ring
that hangs above
our heads, just out
of reach
but always

in full view …

Their love
and sacrifice
sleepless nights
fear-filled days
adding weight
so heavy that every step
toward the promise
leads me closer to
that soft ground, damp
with all the blood and sweat
from riders before me
spilling down
back to that earth.

Abuelitas

I love when the abuelitas,
with a thousand sunrises
in their eyes and endless
memories folded into the
arrugas in their caramelo
skin, smile and tell me they
love my woven bag

an oversized bolsa, slung
easily across my body,
turquoise and golden threads
forming golden amapolas -
my favorite - intricately folded
by weathered hands,
hands the color of the earth

I imagine myself as an
abuelita, a lifetime of
knowledge in my eyes, hands
gnarled like tree roots from
weaving stories and smiles
drying herbs of our past
and creating teas for
our futures
trying to live

up to the lives created
and forged by my abuelita
before me and her abuelita
en los montes de Durango.

Two Ingredients

The comal heats up on
the gas stove, readying itself
to take a short stack of
tortillas de maíz, the yellow
pores emitting the smell
of childhood, of early morning
breakfast, my mom's laughter
as my dad cracked a joke,
flipping it over with her
hand, the tortilla hardening,
my sister and I waiting
for the best part ...
queso quesito rico
calientito apapachado in
between the toasted maíz.

Divorce

Sitting on this couch
gray like used up coal
shifting my weight
searching for comfort
instead, the metal frame
digging into my thighs
leaving an imprint
I'm facing the wrong way

The room is still
the house is quiet
the air is dry,
dust particles
suspended in the air
never dropping

I stare out at the walls
a creamy, whipped avocado
left out too late, spoiled,
a rank taste in my mouth

There are perfect square holes
rectangles and parallelograms
a geometry of empty
spaces that used to be

captured memories

Memories disappeared,
a heaviness like
falling in your sleep and
not being able to wake,
a muffled scream that
can never make it past
the tightness in your
throat before a good cry

That bitter taste of avocado
once again reminding you
of that choice to taste
even after leaving it out
knowing it would be rancid
but hopeful it would still be
creamy, caressing the inside
of your mouth, nourishing
instead, making you sick.

Knowing Touch

You place your hands
on my shoulders
cover nearly every inch
of my brown skin
with their expansiveness
fingertips pressing
deep into my tissue

Your strength injected
working out knots
filled with centuries
of struggle, survival
bridled anger
collected over the
eons, resting just under
the surface, like
magma bubbling, hot
waiting for its moment
to burst out, explode

The sorrow and grief
of losing myself, over
and over to all those
around me, to the small
boxes I was told to stay

in, the boxes they put
mi amá y apá, my
ancestors and me

Lakes of tears stored
from holding back
holding in all that
emotion for fear of
judgment, of exposing
my tenderness

I close my eyes and feel
your body, your self
pouring into me through
those knowing digits,
your gentle intention,
understanding
of the human anatomy
and me,

You begin to release
each lake, each pool
back into my bloodstream,
the air stream, to be
absorbed back into who I
am, and who I'm letting go.

Yellow Kernels in a Dish

The sweetness mingles with the salty,
the spice and the sour.

I close my eyes, savor it.

When my child was little, I'd pick her up
after school and bring her home.
We live across the street from an
elementary school and every day,
there was a man with a cart
selling elotes elotitos
to the students and parents alike.

My child was convinced
the man was there just for her.

I'd buy a single elote,
smothered in mayo, butter,
grated cheese and spices
aromas eliciting the juices
in our mouths to spill out.
We'd sit on the red steps
of our house, she and I,
and take turns, the cheese
dusting the ground

below us, the mayo
dripping from the corners
of our lips.

As she got older,
she asked for his own.

This elote did not come
on a stick from a street vendor,
instead was served at a restaurant
downtown, shared with a woman,
a sister with a warm smile
and matching caramelo skin
she reminded me of
my daughter, echoed the memory
and while a dish replaced
the stick, the taste
was just as sweet.

In the Night

My cat's yowls pierced
the stillness
of my house tonight.

Her guttural calls, full of ache
low and deep
echo against the walls
and are left
unanswered.

I hear her pacing, slow
across the worn carpets
waiting for a lover
who never comes.

Colors

Her insides
scream
in every color of the rainbow
it only makes sense that those
colors make
an appearance
in the change
of her hair.

Drowning

I've been treading water
so long that my legs are
numb and my fingers are
puckered and shriveled
like watery raisins

My breath is shallow
and my arms, outstretched
in front of me, holding her
so she can breathe easy
the muscles in them are
taut, with no give left,
dangerously approach
breaking, spasms shaking

My grip, my head goes under
your hands at the crown
pushing me down so you
can stay above the surface

My arms stay true
but I widen my stare
deafened by the echoes
of my heartbeat
underwater.

Day Trip

We ride in the car
through the windy mountain road
your laughter fills the space
and I bask in its warmth

As we get deeper and deeper
towering redwoods
with their solid girth
and feathering greens
piercing the sky
they spring up
all around us
and we slow down

Take it in
take it up
get lost
together.

Sunday

Today, I sit at a wooden
picnic table, sundress to match
the sunny day in April, thong
sandals cause I don't plan on
walking, ready to be in
company with a friend for
updates and chisme, but really
the chisme and mimosas
and huaraches with a sunny side
egg dripping all over, knowing
there's no way I could finish it.
Rewind three decades and I
would have been five hours in
to a day of work at La Pulga
closed-toe shoes to protect my
feet if something fell, insoles for all
the walking I'd do and right about
now we'd be sitting in the front cab
of that burnt orange van, eating lunch,
beans and cheese tacos that stuck to our ribs
and made us feel full, longer.

Adequate Love

What is adequate love?
I ask the cold air around me.

Is it the warmth of friendship
stepping together
laughing, sharing, commiserating
filling the space between us
with joyful connection?

Or the quiet comforting embrace
from my mother, now my peer
still filling me with peace
every time, her hands in my hair
braiding the strands together?

Is it the delightful squeal
from my niece as she runs
to greet me, jump in my arms
tell me all about her day in
one breath?

Or the slow, deep purr from
my little gray cat as she cuddles
closer to me on cold mornings
burying herself into my lap, under
my arms, completely content?

Nadia

My sister drags
her paintbrush
like a shooting star
across the canvas
of her sky, effortless
like taking a breath,
falling asleep
blinking a nude-
shadowed eye

Suspirando colores,
pigmented storytelling
a fire burning,
flutters within
her heart
staining the frame
creating life with
every stroke.

Better

'En la mar'
echoes from my portable speaker
Mana transporting me
from my early 40s, a government
job and no wrinkles … yet
a calm in the eye of the storm
to my teenage self, full of
angst and hope and determination

To be something, someone
fulfill my parents' hopes
and dreams of something … better

Confusion and contradictions
straddling the old world and new
how do I hold on to what makes
me, my mom, my abuelita, us
in the pursuit of something … better?

How I wish I could have told
my younger self, relax, let me
fast forward to the end, and
spoiler, you go back to the beginning

My mom's fideo and abuelita's

cafecito de la olla, the smells
of her Ruda y Yerba Buena
what we had was always … better.

Desert Bloom

I watch as you transform,
leaving behind you a dried-up,
shell of your former
asphalt and LED screen self,
with every granite boulder you
scale, every ledge you jump down
from, your muscles grow stronger
recognizing their truth, now
that they aren't burdened with
the monotony of the uniformed
classrooms, the constant standing
in place, sitting still as others speak
you sprout wings, stretching out
with every joke, every guttural laugh
you shine with warmth, with joy
as we run from flora to flora,
cataloging each until we are spent
my sweetest child, you wrap your arm
around mine and walk, the sand and stones
crunching under our feet, remembering
what it's like to be us.

Mexican-American

I am not a Latina
swimming in the seas
of continents and language

I am not a Hispanic
raising the flag of our
colonizer, rapist fathers

I am not a BIPOC
meaningless acronym
further dividing us

I am not a person of color
choosing a crayon from a box
to belong to

I refuse to be watered down
stuffed in a box
made smaller

I refuse to be complicit
in the further siloing
creating artificial teams
of you versus me

I refuse to deny who I am
where I come from
what I am part of

I refuse to deny there's no me
without you
without us

Stop obscuring things.
Stop choking my voice.
Stop casting me into a fog.
Stop pitting us against one another.
STOP.

California

With my golden brown skin
and my dark brown eyes
the soft movement of my hips when I walk by
I am the dream that brought you here.

The colors in my hair
and the joy in my laughter
I am the love you desired.

My awe in the presence of nature
and my appreciation and anticipation of
beauty in art and in people
I am the reflection of all that is good in you.

I am the person you are now
and the person you want to become.

I am your California.

ACKNOWLEDGEMENTS

This is a dream decades in the making. In fact, I remember the 10-year-old version of me, daydreaming at La Pulga during slow moments of what it would be like to be a published author - to be a real writer with books to her name like the names of my favorite authors, in particular Ursula Le Guin and her breathtaking Catwings series. So many people have made this finished product possible. Made this version of me possible.

I want to first thank my editor and designer for your guidance in making this a polished first effort. I want to thank Susan Ellenberg, Jonathan Borca, Anne Ward Ernst, Cat Uong and Derrick Seaver - my best friend - for your unwavering encouragement, your belief in my words and for offering me your reactions, insights and direction. To Rosanna Alvarez, Diana Medina and Mighty Mike McGee for inspiring me to step out into the light with my poetry. To Jacqueline Ramseyer, Liz Nguyen and Vicki Thompson for believing in me. Always. And to my sister from another mister, Kim Boynton, thank you for being a sounding board and my champion for nearly 30 years.

I want to thank my parents, Virginia and Jesus, for their sacrifices, their incredibly hard work and love, my sister, Nadia, for her passion for natural beauty. I want to thank my nieces, Norah and Olivia, for reminding me of joy and delight. And most of all, I want to thank my hermosa, my daughter and love of my life, Avery, for teaching me to be brave.